THIS WORKBOOK

BELONGS TO :

Trace the letters from A to Z with their sentences and practice writing them in the space provided

Then use the blank page to write on your own

A is for

Apple

Trace the cursive letters, then write your own

a a a a a a a a a a a a

a

Trace the cursive letters, then write your own

a a a a a a a a a a a a

a

Trace the cursive sentence, then write it

Adam ate an apple

Use this page to practice what you have learned in the previous one

B is for

Bear

Trace the cursive letters, then write your own

b b b b b b b

b

Trace the cursive letters, then write your own

B B B B B B

B

Trace the cursive sentence, then write it

Brown bears are my favorite

Use this page to practice what you have learned in the previous one

C is for

Cat

Trace the cursive letters, then write your own

c   c   c   c   c   c   c   c   c   c

c

Trace the cursive letters, then write your own

C   C   C   C   C   C   C

C

Trace the cursive sentence, then write it

My cat's name is cassy

Trace the cursive letters, then write your own

d   d   d   d   d   d

d

Trace the cursive letters, then write your own

D   D   D   D   D   D

D

Trace the cursive sentence, then write it

Use this page to practice what you have learned in the previous one

E is for

Elephant

Trace the cursive letters, then write your own

e   e   e   e   e   e   e   e   e

e

Trace the cursive letters, then write your own

E   E   E   E   E   E   E

E

Trace the cursive sentence, then write it

Elephants are so big

Use this page to practice what you have learned in the previous one

Trace the cursive letters, then write your own

Trace the cursive letters, then write your own

Trace the cursive sentence, then write it

G is for
Gloves

Trace the cursive letters, then write your own

g

Trace the cursive letters, then write your own

G

Trace the cursive sentence, then write it

Doctors always wear gloves

Use this page to practice what you have learned in the previous one

Name: _______________________   Date: _______________________

Trace the cursive letters, then write your own

h   h   h   h   h   h   h

h

Trace the cursive letters, then write your own

H   H   H   H   H   H   H

H

Trace the cursive sentence, then write it

Our house is small and clean

Use this page to practice what you have learned in the previous one

Trace the cursive letters, then write your own

i i i i i i i i i

i

Trace the cursive letters, then write your own

l l l l l l l l

l

Trace the cursive sentence, then write it

Ink stains are hard to clean

Use this page to practice what you have learned in the previous one

J is for

Juice

Trace the cursive letters, then write your own

j

Trace the cursive letters, then write your own

J

Trace the cursive sentence, then write it

Do you want orange juice ?

Use this page to practice what you have learned in the previous one

Name: Date:

Trace the cursive letters, then write your own

k   k k k k k k k

k

Trace the cursive letters, then write your own

K   K K K K K K K

K

Trace the cursive sentence, then write it

Use this page to practice what you have learned in the previous one

Trace the cursive letters, then write your own

l l l l l l l l l l

l

Trace the cursive letters, then write your own

L L L L L L L L L L

L

Trace the cursive sentence, then write it

Use this page to practice what you have learned in the previous one

Name: Date:

Trace the cursive letters, then write your own

m   m   m   m   m   m

m

Trace the cursive letters, then write your own

M   m   m   m   m   m

m

Trace the cursive sentence, then write it

This mouse has a pink nose

Use this page to practice what you have learned in the previous one

N is for

Noodles

Trace the cursive letters, then write your own

n   n   n   n   n   n   n

n

Trace the cursive letters, then write your own

n   n   n   n   n   n

n

Trace the cursive sentence, then write it

I prepared noodles for lunch

Use this page to practice what you have learned in the previous one

Name: **Date:**

Trace the cursive letters, then write your own

O O O O O O O O

O

Trace the cursive letters, then write your own

O O O O O O O O

O

Trace the cursive sentence, then write it

The owl is a nocturnal animal

Use this page to practice what you have learned in the previous one

Name: Date:

Trace the cursive letters, then write your own

p

Trace the cursive letters, then write your own

P

Trace the cursive sentence, then write it

Use this page to practice what you have learned in the previous one

Trace the cursive letters, then write your own

Trace the cursive letters, then write your own

Trace the cursive sentence, then write it

Use this page to practice what you have learned in the previous one

Trace the cursive letters, then write your own

Trace the cursive letters, then write your own

Trace the cursive sentence, then write it

S is for
Sun

Trace the cursive letters, then write your own

s   *s   s   s   s   s   s   s*

s

Trace the cursive letters, then write your own

S   S   S   S   S   S   S   S

S

Trace the cursive sentence, then write it

The sun rises from the east

Name: Date:

Trace the cursive letters, then write your own

t   t   t   t   t   t   t

t

Trace the cursive letters, then write your own

T   T   T   T   T   T   T   T

T

Trace the cursive sentence, then write it

Use this page to practice what you have learned in the previous one

Trace the cursive letters, then write your own

u   u   u   u   u   u   u

u

Trace the cursive letters, then write your own

U   U   U   U   U   U

U

Trace the cursive sentence, then write it

Use this page to practice what you have learned in the previous one

Trace the cursive letters, then write your own

V is for Van

Trace the cursive letters, then write your own

Trace the cursive letters, then write your own

Trace the cursive sentence, then write it

Traveling in van is very fun

Use this page to practice what you have learned in the previous one

Trace the cursive letters, then write your own

w   w   w   w   w   w

w

Trace the cursive letters, then write your own

W   W   W   W   W   W

W

Trace the cursive sentence, then write it

Blue whales are giants

Trace the cursive letters, then write your own

x   x   x   x   x   x   x

x

Trace the cursive letters, then write your own

X   X   X   X   X   X

X

Trace the cursive sentence, then write it

Use this page to practice what you have learned in the previous one

Name: ________________________   Date: ________________________

Y is for
Yogurt

Trace the cursive letters, then write your own

y   y   y   y   y   y   y
y

Trace the cursive letters, then write your own

Y   Y   Y   Y   Y   Y
Y

Trace the cursive sentence, then write it

Can I have some yogurt ?

Use this page to practice what you have learned in the previous one

Z is for
Zebra

Trace the cursive letters, then write your own

Z Z Z Z Z Z Z
Z

Trace the cursive letters, then write your own

z z z z z z
z

Trace the cursive sentence, then write it

The Zebra is a special animal

Use this page to practice what you have learned in the previous one

AFTER YOUR PURCHASE, WE WOULD BE SO GRATEFUL IF YOU LEAVE US A REVIEW WITH YOUR EXPERIENCE THIS WILL HELP US TO CONTINUE PUBLISHING BETTER BOOKS, IT ALSO HELPS OTHER PARENTS TO BE SATISFIED